LAYERS OF LEARNING

YEAR ONE • UNIT EIGHT

ASSYRIANS
DESERTS
FLUIDS
RHYTHM

HooDoo Publishing
United States of America
©2014 Layers of Learning
Copies of maps or activities may be made for a particular family or classroom.
ISBN 978-1494791735

Units At A Glance: Topics For All Four Years of the Layers of Learning Program

1	History	Geography	Science	The Arts
1	Mesopotamia	Maps & Globes	Planets	Cave Paintings
2	Egypt	Map Keys	Stars	Egyptian Art
3	Europe	Global Grids	Earth & Moon	Crafts
4	Ancient Greece	Wonders	Satellites	Greek Art
5	Babylon	Mapping People	Humans in Space	Poetry
6	The Levant	Physical Earth	Laws of Motion	List Poems
7	Phoenicians	Oceans	Motion	Moral Stories
8	Assyrians	Deserts	Fluids	Rhythm
9	Persians	Arctic	Waves	Melody
10	Ancient China	Forests	Machines	Chinese Art
11	Early Japan	Mountains	States of Matter	Line & Shape
12	Arabia	Rivers & Lakes	Atoms	Color & Value
13	Ancient India	Grasslands	Elements	Texture & Form
14	Ancient Africa	Africa	Bonding	African Tales
15	First North Americans	North America	Salts	Creative Kids
16	Ancient South America	South America	Plants	South American Art
17	Celts	Europe	Flowering Plants	Jewelry
18	Roman Republic	Asia	Trees	Roman Art
19	Christianity	Australia & Oceania	Simple Plants	Instruments
20	Roman Empire	You Explore	Fungi	Composing Music

2	History	Geography	Science	The Arts
1	Byzantines	Turkey	Climate & Seasons	Byzantine Art
2	Barbarians	Ireland	Forecasting	Illumination
3	Islam	Arabian Peninsula	Clouds & Precipitation	Creative Kids
4	Vikings	Norway	Special Effects	Viking Art
5	Anglo Saxons	Britain	Wild Weather	King Arthur Tales
6	Charlemagne	France	Cells and DNA	Carolingian Art
7	Normans	Nigeria	Skeletons	Canterbury Tales
8	Feudal System	Germany	Muscles, Skin, & Cardiopulmonary	Gothic Art
9	Crusades	Balkans	Digestive & Senses	Religious Art
10	Burgundy, Venice, Spain	Switzerland	Nerves	Oil Paints
11	Wars of the Roses	Russia	Health	Minstrels & Plays
12	Eastern Europe	Hungary	Metals	Printmaking
13	African Kingdoms	Mali	Carbon Chem	Textiles
14	Asian Kingdoms	Southeast Asia	Non-metals	Vivid Language
15	Mongols	Caucasus	Gases	Fun With Poetry
16	Medieval China & Japan	China	Electricity	Asian Arts
17	Pacific Peoples	Micronesia	Circuits	Arts of the Islands
18	American Peoples	Canada	Technology	Indian Legends
19	The Renaissance	Italy	Magnetism	Renaissance Art I
20	Explorers	Caribbean Sea	Motors	Renaissance Art II

3	History	Geography	Science	The Arts
1	Age of Exploration	Argentina and Chile	Classification & Insects	Fairy Tales
2	The Ottoman Empire	Egypt and Libya	Reptiles & Amphibians	Poetry
3	Mogul Empire	Pakistan & Afghanistan	Fish	Mogul Arts
4	Reformation	Angola & Zambia	Birds	Reformation Art
5	Renaissance England	Tanzania & Kenya	Mammals & Primates	Shakespeare
6	Thirty Years' War	Spain	Sound	Baroque Music
7	The Dutch	Netherlands	Light & Optics	Baroque Art I
8	France	Indonesia	Bending Light	Baroque Art II
9	The Enlightenment	Korean Pen.	Color	Art Journaling
10	Russia & Prussia	Central Asia	History of Science	Watercolors
11	Conquistadors	Baltic States	Igneous Rocks	Creative Kids
12	Settlers	Peru & Bolivia	Sedimentary Rocks	Native American Art
13	13 Colonies	Central America	Metamorphic Rocks	Settler Sayings
14	Slave Trade	Brazil	Gems & Minerals	Colonial Art
15	The South Pacific	Australasia	Fossils	Principles of Art
16	The British in India	India	Chemical Reactions	Classical Music
17	Boston Tea Party	Japan	Reversible Reactions	Folk Music
18	Founding Fathers	Iran	Compounds & Solutions	Rococo
19	Declaring Independence	Samoa and Tonga	Oxidation & Reduction	Creative Crafts I
20	The American Revolution	South Africa	Acids & Bases	Creative Crafts II

4	History	Geography	Science	The Arts
1	American Government	USA	Heat & Temperature	Patriotic Music
2	Expanding Nation	Pacific States	Motors & Engines	Tall Tales
3	Industrial Revolution	U.S. Landscapes	Energy	Romantic Art I
4	Revolutions	Mountain West States	Energy Sources	Romantic Art II
5	Africa	U.S. Political Maps	Energy Conversion	Impressionism I
6	The West	Southwest States	Earth Structure	Impressionism II
7	Civil War	National Parks	Plate Tectonics	Post-Impressionism
8	World War I	Plains States	Earthquakes	Expressionism
9	Totalitarianism	U.S. Economics	Volcanoes	Abstract Art
10	Great Depression	Heartland States	Mountain Building	Kinds of Art
11	World War II	Symbols and Landmarks	Chemistry of Air & Water	War Art
12	Modern East Asia	The South States	Food Chemistry	Modern Art
13	India's Independence	People of America	Industry	Pop Art
14	Israel	Appalachian States	Chemistry of Farming	Modern Music
15	Cold War	U.S. Territories	Chemistry of Medicine	Free Verse
16	Vietnam War	Atlantic States	Food Chains	Photography
17	Latin America	New England States	Animal Groups	Latin American Art
18	Civil Rights	Home State Study	Instincts	Theater & Film
19	Technology	Home State Study II	Habitats	Architecture
20	Terrorism	America in Review	Conservation	Creative Kids

Unit 1-8 Printable Pack

This unit includes printables at the end. To make life easier for you we also created digital printable packs for each unit. To retrieve your printable pack for Unit 1-8, please visit

www.layers-of-learning.com/digital-printable-packs/

Put the printable pack in your shopping cart and use this coupon code:

1223UNIT1-8

Your printable pack will be free.

LAYERS OF LEARNING INTRODUCTION

This is part of a series of units in the Layers of Learning homeschool curriculum, including the subjects of history, geography, science, and the arts. Children from 1st through 12th can participate in the same curriculum at the same time - family school style.

The units are intended to be used in order as the basis of a complete curriculum (once you add in a systematic math, reading, and writing program). You begin with Year 1 Unit 1 no matter what ages your children are. Spend about 2 weeks on each unit. You pick and choose the activities within the unit that appeal to you and read the books from the book list that are available to you or find others on the same topic from your library. We highly recommend that you use the timeline in every history section as the backbone. Then flesh out your learning with reading and activities that highlight the topics you think are the most important.

Alternatively, you can use the units as activity ideas to supplement another curriculum in any order you wish. You can still use them with all ages of children at the same time.

When you've finished with Year One, move on to Year Two, Year Three, and Year Four. Then begin again with Year One and work your way through the years again. Now your children will be older, reading more involved books, and writing more in depth. When you have completed the sequence for the second time, you start again on it for the third and final time. If your student began with Layers of Learning in 1st grade and stayed with it all the way through she would go through the four year rotation three times, firmly cementing the information in her mind in ever increasing depth. At each level you should expect increasing amounts of outside reading and writing. High schoolers in particular should be reading extensively, and if possible, participating in discussion groups.

☺ ☻ ☻ These icons will guide you in spotting activities and books that are appropriate for the age of child you are working with. But if you think an activity is too juvenile or too difficult for your kids, adjust accordingly. The icons are not there as rules, just guides.

☺ GRADES 1-4

☻ GRADES 5-8

☻ GRADES 9-12

Within each unit we share:
- EXPLORATIONS, activities relating to the topic;
- EXPERIMENTS, usually associated with science topics;
- EXPEDITIONS, field trips;
- EXPLANATIONS, teacher helps or educational philosophies.

In the sidebars we also include Additional Layers, Famous Folks, Fabulous Facts, On the Web, and other extra related topics that can take you off on tangents, exploring the world and your interests with a bit more freedom. The curriculum will always be there to pull you back on track when you're ready.

You can learn more about how to use this curriculum at www.layers-of-learning.com/layers-of-learning-program/

UNIT EIGHT

ASSYRIANS – DESERTS – FLUIDS – RHYTHM

It is easier to build strong children than to repair broken men.
-Frederick Douglass

	LIBRARY LIST:
HISTORY	Search for: Assyrians, Nineveh, Ashurbanipal, Mesopotamia ☺ ☻ <u>How the Amazon Queen Fought the Prince of Egypt</u> by Tamara Bower. Re-told from an ancient Assyrian legend. ☺ ☻ <u>Famous Figures of Ancient Times</u> by Cathy Diez-Luckie. Punch-out paper dolls of ancients, including Assyrians, but also Egyptians, Phoenicians, Israelites, Romans and more. Colored and black and white versions of each paper figure. Short biographies accompany. ☺ ☻ <u>The Ancient Near Eastern World</u>. Covers the major Middle Eastern civilizations, their interactions, and what we've inherited from them. Study guide available. ☻ ☻ <u>The Assyrian Empire</u> by Don Nardo. ☻ <u>The Babylonian Story of the Deluge As Told By Assyrian Tablets From Nineveh</u> by E.A. Wallis Budge.
GEOGRAPHY	Search for: Deserts, Sonora, Sahara, Kalahari, Gobi, Atacama, Arabian Desert ☺ <u>Creatures of the Desert</u> from the National Geographic Society. Moveable tabs and pictures for young kids to learn and play at the same time. ☺ <u>Cactus Desert, One Small Square</u> by Donald Silver. Get an entire picture of the ecosystem by keeping a close eye on one square foot. ☺ ☻ <u>A Walk in the Desert</u> by Rebecca L. Johnson. Focuses on the Sonoran Desert. ☺ ☻ <u>One Day in the Desert</u> by Jean Craighead George. A fictional account of a coming desert storm and the people and animals who have to find shelter. Takes place in the Sonoran Desert of southwest America. ☻ <u>101 Questions About Desert Life</u> by Alice Jablonsky. Each page is a new question about the desert. Answers are fairly detailed and use some technical language. Focuses on the American southwestern deserts. ☻ <u>Explore the Desert</u> by Kay Jackson. Absolutely perfect overview of desert biomes, simple vocabulary and sentence structure makes it accessible to less experienced readers as well. ☻ ☻ <u>52 Days By Camel</u> by Lawrie Raskin and Debora Pearson. Chronicles the actual trip taken by Raskin across the Sahara Desert. Fascinating side notes into the people and places along the way. ☻ ☻ <u>The Sonoran Desert by Day and Night</u> by Dot Barlowe. A very detailed coloring book from Dover. Each picture is accompanied with a short description. ☺ ☻ ☻ <u>Deserts of the Earth</u> by Michael Martin. Photographs of people, landforms and life of the deserts from one who has traveled through the world's driest places.

SCIENCE

Search for: fluids, liquids, gases, density, pressure, buoyancy, submarines

☺ Who Sank The Boat by Pamela Allen. A host of animals climb into the boat and finally a tiny mouse sinks the boat. Use this story as an introduction to dive into an exploration of the physics of fluids.

☺ What Floats? What Sinks? A Look at Density by Jennifer Boothroyd.

☺ The Way Things Move by Heidi Gold-Dwarkin. An experiment book for the very young.

☺ Fun With Water and Bubbles by Heidi Gold-Dwarkin. Experiments covering all the basics of fluids.

☺ Dive! Dive! Dive!: Buoyancy by Isabel Thomas. Discusses buoyancy in the context of submarines.

☺ Experiments With Water by Chris Oxlade. Covers more than just the physics of fluids.

☺ A+ Projects in Physics by Janice Van Cleave. Use this all through the physics sections in all the years of this program. Van Cleave books are always worth keeping on hand.

☺ ☺ Liquids and Gases: Principles of Fluid Mechanics by Paul Fleisher. Covers the essential principles of fluid physics with diagrams and illustrations, plus activities to try.

THE ARTS

Search for: rhythm, drums, beat, percussion

☺ Hand, Hand, Fingers Thumb by Al Perkins. Classic story where rhythm and drumming are the main feature. So much fun to read aloud.

☺ Max Found Two Sticks by Brian Pinkney. A boy sits on the front steps of his house making music with sticks and make-shift drums. The story is told in fascinating rhythm.

☺ The Jazz Fly by Matthew Golub. Told in magical lyrical rhythm, look for the version with the CD for the full music experience.

☺ ☺ Miss Mary Mack by Mary Ann Hoberman. A book you are supposed to clap along with. Look up the history of this rhythm hand clap.

☺ ☺ The Book of Rhythms by Langston Hughes. Written by a famous American poet, this book helps kids hear the rhythms in everyday life and translate that into music and poetry.

☺ Alfred's Kid's Drum Course, Bk 1 by Dave Black. A total beginner's drum course if you have a child inclined that way.

☺ ☺ ☺ Slap Happy: How To Play World Beat Rhythms With Just Your Body and a Buddy by Alan Dworsky and Betty Sansby. Hand clapping games to do with a friend. Besides teaching rhythm, you get a musical tour of the world with this book.

☺ A Rhythmic Vocabulary: A Musicians Guide to Understanding and Improvising With Rhythm by Alan Dworsky and Betty Sansby. For people who are already serious about music and want to really understand rhythm.

HISTORY: ASSYRIANS

Additional Layer
This fantastical beast was carved to guard the city of Nimrud. It is called a lamassu. You'll find a coloring sheet of one in the printables section. Learn more about magical beasts that people make up. Make up your own guardian on the next printable.

Assyria was originally a small country up north on the Tigris River that featured the cities of Nineveh, Nimrud, and Ashur. The Assyrian Empire eventually spread over most of Mesopotamia and much of Egypt. They worshiped a god called Ashur (among others) and named one of their cities after him. They believed their king was directly appointed by the god Ashur and spoke for the god. When a government claims a direct mandate from a god, we call this a theocracy. The people must obey or they risk not only this life but the next as well.

If you were an Assyrian, then summer was war season. They went out every year to gain more lands and conquer more people. Of course, those people didn't like being conquered, so they would resist and rebel. The Assyrians looked down on rebellion and punished offenders with a general sacking and burning of their cities. If you wanted peace more than freedom, you just paid the Assyrians a tribute every year.

Fabulous Fact
Everybody has a look, here's the Assyrian head gear . . . so stylin' in Nineveh this year.

☺ ☺ ☻ **EXPLORATION: Assyrian Timeline**
Make a timeline of ancient Assyria. Start with these dates:
- 2000 BC Assyrian Kingdom established
- 1220 BC Babylon comes under the control of Assyria
- 1000-663 BC Assyrian Kingdom grows into an empire
- 883-859 BC King Ashurbanipal II is king of Assyria, and the city of Nimrud is built
- 841 BC Israel is paying tribute to Assyria
- 704-681 BC King Sennacherib builds Nineveh
- 701 BC Sennacherib defeats most of Israel, but fails to take the capital city, Jerusalem
- 671 BC Assyrians conquer Egypt
- 612-609 BC Babylonians and Medes defeat Assyria at Carchemish and the empire falls.

☺ ☺ ☺ EXPLORATION: Map of Assyria

Make a map of the Assyrian Empire using the map from the end of this unit.

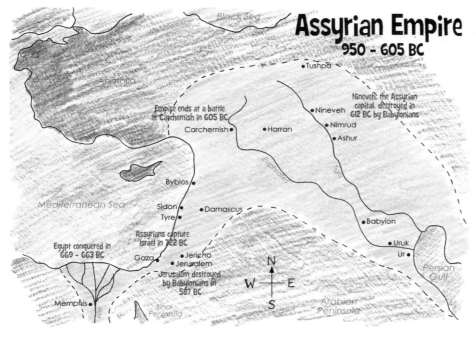

☺ ☺ EXPLORATION: The King's Chariot

The Assyrians used chariots in war, which is one of the things that made them so formidable. Make a model chariot out of a small paper box (like a milk carton or something similar), two round lids (like milk jug lids), and wooden skewer for an axle. Punch a hole through the box and both lids, and run the skewer through to attach the wheels. Use a pipe cleaner attached to the front for the tongue. Since you're making the king's chariot, you need to give it a special paint job. Paint it gold and cover it with sequins and plastic gemstones for precious stones. Make it as fancy as you like.

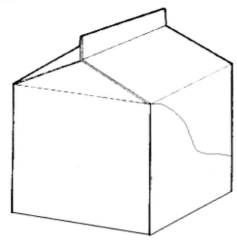

Draw a line like this one and cut along it to form the sides of the chariot.

Famous Folks

Ashurbanipal: the good, the bad, and the ugly.

On the one hand, he created a magnificent library that still exists today and he was much loved by his subjects. On the other hand, his cruelty and harshness toward his enemies makes the top ten in evil rulers of the world. As for the ugly, well, look at that beard!

Writer's Workshop

Consider the dangers of having a theocratic government. The Puritans of colonial America exercised this type of government. *The Crucible* by Arthur Miller tells the story of the Salem Witch Trials during that time period. Read the play, then write about theocracies both in ancient times and modern.

Additional Layer

The study of fashion in history is fascinating. Here is a picture of an Assyrian commoner, court official and two noblemen. Learn more about what the Assyrians wore, including hairstyles.

Fabulous Fact
No culture is an island. The Assyrians were heavily influenced by those who came before as well as their neighbors. And, in turn, the Assyrians did a lot of influencing themselves. We really can't know where many of the traditions of these people first started, but it is fascinating to see how they overlap. For example, the Assyrians believed in a powerful figure who was the sole survivor, with his family, of a great flood. They also prohibited all work on the seventh day of every week.

☺ ☻ EXPLORATION: Battering Ram

We know the Assyrians were often at war; now you get to build one of the war weapons they used. Because ancient cities were so often surrounded by huge city walls, it was difficult for armies to get in to attack the target city. Battering rams were used to force open the doors or put a hole through the wall so the armies could get in. The simplest form of a battering ram was just a tree trunk. A group of men picked up the tree trunk and rammed it into the city wall over and over again until they broke through. Often the tip of the battering ram was reinforced with metal so it would be stronger and do more damage.

Build a battering ram using:
- a cardboard paper towel tube
- newspaper scraps
- foil
- duct tape

Start by filling the paper towel tube with as many newspaper scraps as you can fit inside. This is to make it solid and strong. Now cut a square of foil and surround one of the ends with the foil. You may want to use several layers of foil.

Now surround the entire thing with duct tape until it's totally covered, leaving only the foil tip showing.

Try your battering ram out by building a tower or wall with blocks and then knocking it down with your battering ram.

☺ ☻ EXPLORATION: Shaduf

Besides going to war, the Assyrians were also farmers. They grew fruits, vegetables, and barley. They didn't get enough rain to keep their crops watered though, so they used a special irrigation tool called a

shaduf. It was a hand-operated irrigation device that could lift water from a river into the canal systems they built for watering their crops. They dunked the bucket into the water and then, once it was full, lifted it out and dumped it in a canal. It was much easier than lifting a normal bucket because of the long pole and counterweight. The Assyrians were not the only people to use shadufs. The Egyptians, eastern Europeans, and many Asian cultures all used, and still use, this device.

To make a shaduf, you'll need:
- 8 craft sticks
- 2 small sticks (we used rounded chopsticks)
- a small plastic cup
- a piece of clay (about the size of a golf ball)
- a piece of string or yard (about 2 feet long)
- hot glue and glue gun

First, make the structure with the eight craft sticks. Triangular legs make a strong support. You can use hot glue and string to secure the joints. Next, fasten string around a small cup at one end and around a small stick at the other end. The clay will sit on the opposite end of that stick. You may need to adjust the amount of clay for the right balance. We also used bits of clay to act as the "ground" that the legs sat on. Set up some containers of water and practice scooping, moving, and pouring the water.

*This same project can be done on a larger scale near a river, pond, lake, or creek. Use a full size bucket and large sticks or logs secured with ropes. Any object that will stay on the logs (like a rock lashed to the sticks with a rope) will work for the counterweight on top.

Additional Layer

The city of Nineveh is shown on this map.

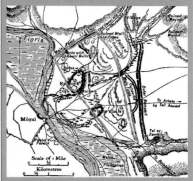

The city walls are in brown, the Tigris River is blue, and farmland is shown in green. The city is at the modern day site of Mosul, Iraq. Look it up on a map.

Additional Layer

They didn't play football and basketball in ancient Assyria; they went on lion hunts! They did this to show off and to practice their skills so they would be ready to go to war and fight. Usually, soldiers with shields stood in a circle to keep the lion in (like an arena made of men!). Then the king would ride in and spear the lion.

Additional Layer

Alexander the Great, upon seeing the marvelous library at Nineveh, decided to build one of his own. He died before the project got off the ground though. It was left to his general, Ptolemy, to establish the famed Library of Alexandria in Egypt.

Fabulous Fact

"Corn" in ancient times didn't mean the yellow kernels that grow on a cob. The word meant any kind of seed grain that people dried and ground up to make flour. The corn we are familiar with is purely American and was unknown to the ancients of Mesopotamia and the Mediterranean.

☺ ☻ EXPLORATION: "King of the Universe"

Assyrian kings believed they were chosen by god to rule and that conquering other people was just part of their job, which explains why they spent so much time at war. They gave themselves really intimidating sounding names to make all the people fear or revere them.

Make a list of your nicknames in your writer's notebook. What do your parents and friends call you?

Now come up with some new names for yourself. What would you call yourself if:

- you wanted someone to be afraid of you?
- you wanted someone to laugh at you?
- you wanted someone to know you are sad or happy?
- you wanted someone to know about one of your great talents?

☺ ☻ ☻ EXPLORATION: Stele

A stele is a standing stone that has an inscription on it. It is usually taller than it is wide. Steles were used for lots of reasons – to record stories and history, to commemorate an important event, or as geographical markers for a boundary or a special place. Some grave markers are steles.

There was a stele found at Asher that told of an Assyrian Queen with this inscription:

> Stele of Sammurammat
> Queen of Shamshi-Adad
> King of all, King of Ashur
> Mother of Adad-nerar;
> King of all, King of Ashur
> Daughter-in-law of Shalmaneser
> King of the four regions.

If there were a stele written about you, what would it say? Make a stele out of a large piece of paper or cardboard. Paint or color it gray like a stone, and then write your personal inscription on it. For ideas on what to say check out the Poetry section of Unit 1-5 where you'll find lots of poetry ideas featuring people.

☺ ☺ ☻ EXPEDITION: Library

The palace at Nineveh had an amazing library. Not only did it contain many famous ancient works, like the Epic of Gilgamesh and Babylonian proverbs, but everything in the library was also organized by subject matter – history, government, religion and music, geography, science, and poetry. There was even a top secret section for classified secret documents.

Go visit your local library and ask for a tour from one of the librarians. Find out how our libraries are organized. Go to http://www.layers-of-learning.com/library-outings/ for some printable library outing activities. The library scavenger hunt worksheet is also included in the printables section at the end of this unit.

Library Scavenger Hunt — Find all 15 items

A cookbook	A book about an artist	A book from the **921** non-fiction section
A board book for babies	An atlas	A fairy tale
A graphic novel	A medieval history book	Someone typing on a computer
Your favorite book	A science book	A sci-fi book about space
A clock	A library card	An encyclopedia set

☺ ☺ EXPLORATION: Ritual of Tammuz

Each fall when it was time to sow the grain, the Assyrian women did a special ritual to appease the god, Tammuz, who was the god of corn. They wept to mourn the death of Tammuz, then threw corn seeds into the ground to die. Of course, the corn didn't really die. They were actually planting the seeds. In their minds, Tammuz blessed them by coming back to life as corn year after year, providing them with food. Really, they were planting the corn seeds on their own!

You can sow corn too. Just find a patch of ground and bury a few corn seeds. You may need to water them a bit, but you should see corn plants coming up within a couple of weeks.

☺ ☺ EXPLORATION: Assyria vs. Hezekiah, Grudge Match of the Millennium

The Assyrians went to war with everybody in the region and so, of course, King Hezekiah of the Jews was on the list. And nobody beat the Assyrians when they were at the top of their game. Hezekiah ruled over a miniscule land called Israel sandwiched in a dry desert region between the Philistines on the one hand and the nomadic desert wanderers on the other. They were easy pickings; or so the Assyrians thought. A famous western poet named Lord Byron wrote a poem about the battle:

Additional Layer

There are still Assyrians today. Many Assyrians converted to Christianity between the first and third centuries. They have a different culture, language, and religion than most of the people who surround them in the Middle East. Because of this, they have suffered and been persecuted throughout the ages. Thousands were killed during World Wars I and II.

Memorization Station

Memorize *The Destruction of Sennacherib* by Byron.

Fabulous Fact

The Assyrian troops probably prayed to Ashur, god of war, before the battle.

Some other Assyrian deities included:

Adad, the weather god

Mah, the earth goddess

and Mutu, god of the underworld.

Writer's Workshop

Authors and poets have often written about times of war. Something about tragedy, bravery, and a cause stirs up our souls.

Go online and look at pictures of recent wars and conflicts in the world, then write about them.

You might write a poem, a reaction paragraph, a letter to an involved politician, a letter for a soldier or war veteran, or an opinion paper.

Additional Layer

2 Kings 17: 16 discusses how the children of Israel had begun to worship graven images instead of their god. What could parallel those ancient graven images in our modern society?

The Destruction of Sennacherib

The Assyrian came down like the wolf on the fold,
And his cohorts were gleaming in purple and gold;
And the sheen of their spears was like stars on the sea,
When the blue wave rolls nightly on deep Galilee.

Like the leaves of the forest when Summer is green,
That host with their banners at sunset were seen:
Like the leaves of the forest when Autumn hath blown,
That host on the morrow lay withered and strown.

For the Angel of Death spread his wings on the blast,
And breathed in the face of the foe as he passed;
And the eyes of the sleepers waxed deadly and chill,
And their hearts but once heaved, and for ever grew still!

And there lay the steed with his nostril all wide,
But through it there rolled not the breath of his pride;
And the foam of his gasping lay white on the turf,
And cold as the spray of the rock-beating surf.

And there lay the rider distorted and pale,
With the dew on his brow, and the rust on his mail:
And the tents were all silent, the banners alone,
The lances unlifted, the trumpet unblown.

And the widows of Ashur are loud in their wail,
And the idols are broke in the temple of Baal;
And the might of the Gentile, unsmote by the sword,
Hath melted like snow in the glance of the Lord!

– George Gordon, Lord Byron

You can read the account of this battle as recorded by the Jews in the Bible (2 Kings 17-18).

GEOGRAPHY: DESERTS

Deserts are defined as places on Earth that get less than 10 inches (250 ml) of precipitation in a year. Deserts are dry. Some deserts are hot and rocky or sandy. Other deserts are in a temperate climate that has cold winters; these deserts are still hot in the summer. Then there are the polar deserts, which are frozen and extremely cold year round.

Hoggar Desert, Algeria. Photo by Florence Devouard, CC license.

The lack of rain and snow fall means that deserts actually lose more water through evaporation than they gain through precipitation in most years. This means deserts have fewer plants and animals than other places on Earth. They also usually have fewer people. Some deserts are so barren that they are almost "dead." Others are known as green deserts, because they have a varied and spectacular wildlife scene. All deserts have at least some life which can survive in this extreme environment.

Deserts usually form where they do because of a rain shadow from nearby mountains. This means that mountains are between the desert and the prevailing winds from the ocean. As the air rises over the mountains it cools and the rain is dropped on the windward side of the mountains, leaving the leeward side dry and barren.

Famous Folks

T.E. Lawrence was an archaeologist who, before and during during WWI, was used by and later enlisted into the British Army. He worked in the deserts of the Middle East and intimately knew the languages and culture of the tribal nomadic wanderers who live there. He, along with the indomitable Gertrude Bell, were essential to the shape and condition of the modern nations in the Middle East.

Oddly, Lawrence was responsible for the modern use of motorcycle helmets. Find out why.

Additional Layer

Learn about some of the native people who live in the Sonoran Desert, like the Hopi or the Navajo.

Fabulous Fact

About one sixth of the population of the world lives in deserts.

Nomads making lunch in the desert.

Additional Layer

Deserts are a type of ecosystem. Talk about the concepts of ecosystem and biome.

Oasis in the Desert by Antal Ligeti

☺ ☺ ☻ **EXPLORATION: Desert Features**

To learn about deserts with kids from kindergarten through 8th grade, start by talking about some of the features of a desert. Make a list together of things and conditions you might find in the desert. Older kids should come having read a book or two on deserts first. You can also read aloud a book or a few pages of a book on deserts to younger kids. Make a web chart or brainstorming poster of everything you know. As you read, add more desert facts. Color the poster to look like a desert as well.

☺ ☺ ☻ **EXPLORATION: Deserts of the World Map**

Use the Deserts of the World map from the end of this unit. Color and label the major deserts of Earth.

Deserts of the World

Label these deserts: Atacama, Sahara, Kalahari, Gobi, Arabian, Thar, Great Victoria, and Sonoran.

Layers of Learning

☻ ☻ ☻ EXPLORATION: Desert Animals

Many animals live in the desert. They are perfectly suited for their environment. Their bodies retain and reuse moisture. They can both get more moisture from food than other animals, and they also conserve it by restricting their activity to the night time in most cases. Read up on one of these desert animals and then make a craft.

Here's an idea for two animals from the Sonoran Desert in America: the Arizona coral snake and the kangaroo rat. Make a paper chain snake being careful to get the pattern correct. There are copycat snakes that look similar but have a different pattern. Add a forked tongue and draw on eyes with a white crayon. Then make a little paper chain Kangaroo rat from two shorter strips of paper (half the length, but the same width as the snake papers). Add ears, a tail and draw on eyes and a nose.

Here are some facts about the animals:

Coral Snake:

- It has a black head and then stripes in this order: yellow, black, yellow, red, yellow, black, yellow, red, yellow, black . . . etc. The black and red stripes never touch on the true coral snake.
- It is the most venomous snake in the Sonoran Desert.
- It is shy and hard to find, so it rarely bites people.
- It comes out only at night to hunt in the cooler temperatures.
- Its favorite prey is the blind snake.

Additional Layer

We chose the snake and rat on purpose because they are predator and prey. You can use them to talk about food chains.

Additional Layer

Find some cactus in the grocery store and eat it.

Additional Layer

The coral snake's colors make a pattern. Talk about patterns with younger kids.

Use pattern blocks, toys, blocks, or other similar objects to create simple patterns with little ones.

Additional Layer

The Gobi Desert in Asia is a cold desert. Antarctica is also a desert.

Fill a cake pan with 1/8 cup of salt for every fact you learn about one of these cold deserts. Then play and write words in your white "desert."

Additional Layer

Learn about some endangered desert animals, like this ocelot.

Additional Layer

What kind of homes do people live in in the desert? How are they different from homes in a northern climate with heavy snowy winters or a tropical wet climate?

Fabulous Fact

Animals that live in the desert have special features or habits that help them survive.

Camels can store water and fat in their hump. Desert mice can get all the water they need from seeds and bugs that they eat. Some animals (like toads) bury themselves deep underground when it is dry, coming out only when the desert rains hit.

- Here's a rhyme to remember which is the dangerous snake: "Red touches black, poison he lack. Red touches yellow, dangerous fellow."

Kangaroo Rat:

- It never needs to drink water. All its moisture comes from the food it eats.
- It eats only seeds.
- It has powerful hind legs and jumps just like a kangaroo.
- It is most active at night.
- It has to watch out for owls, lizards, snakes, coyotes, and small cats like the bobcat.

On each of the yellow and red sections of the snake's body write a fact about the Sonoran Desert or deserts in general.

☺ ☺ ☺ **EXPLORATION: Adventure Map**

First, start by talking about what a desert is, where they are located, and some of the things you might find in a desert. This would be great time to read a book about deserts like Cactus Desert: One Small Square. Make a list together as a group.

Then have the kids draw an adventure map of a desert. They should include some of the plants, animals; and land forms that you discussed. Have them also label places on their map and make a key and a compass rose.

Afterward they can share their map with everyone and tell about their work.

☺ ☺ ☺ **EXPEDITION: Sahara Desert**

This is an armchair expedition. Have the kids pack a bag for their trip (including snacks will make them very happy), park them on the couch and turn on a movie about deserts. The movie "Deserts" from the Planet Earth series by Discovery Channel is excellent. Afterward you can have them write about deserts, find the Sahara Desert on a map, or do another project.

☺ ☺ ☻ **EXPLORATION: Arroyos, Playas, and Dunes**

Deserts have landforms that are unique. Much of the land of deserts is shaped by wind erosion rather than water erosion. In addition, softer areas of sandstone wear away much more quickly than metamorphic rocks, leaving fascinating features like the <u>hoodoos</u> of Southern Utah's deserts. Sandy deserts can form large <u>sand dunes</u> where the wind drifts the sand into piles. Large areas of sand dunes that persist in a particular are are called <u>ergs</u>. Deserts also often have bare

Hoodoos in Bryce Canyon, Utah. Photo by Jonathan Zander.

rock, called <u>yardangs</u>, where the wind has blown the sand and dirt away from the bedrock. <u>Arroyos</u>, <u>dry gulches</u>, and <u>wadis</u> are all different names for dry stream beds which fill up in the occasional torrential rains. Lakes that form for a short time, leaving behind salt and debris deposits are called <u>playas</u>. Playas sometimes turn into <u>salt flats</u>. <u>Mesas</u> are large flat topped rises of land with steep sides. <u>Buttes</u> are like mesas, but smaller. An <u>oasis</u> is an area in the desert where ground water bubbles to the surface, creating an area of fertile green in the middle of the brown desert. Some oases are tiny and others are large enough to support entire towns.

Make your own desert landform book. Find images online or from a magazine, or draw your own of each type of desert landform. Put each one on its own page. Label it and write the definition. Older kids can do their own research and writing. Younger kids can just cut and paste pre-printed pictures and definitions onto their pages.

☺ ☻ ☻ **EXPLORATION: Desert Notebooking**

Create a notebook or lapbook about deserts. There is one notebooking page in the printables at the end of this unit to get you started. Keep your maps in your notebook as well. Choose a desert animal or two to notebook about, and also find out more about at least one specific desert in the world. Research weather, climate, people, animals, plant life, and geographical features, and include them all in your notebook.

Additional Layer

Review or learn about compass roses and keys on maps.

Additional Layer

What are some survival skills you would need if you were traveling in a desert?

These U.S. Navy sailors are learning how to get clean potable water through evaporation.

Writer's Workshop

Write some desert similes. A simile is a comparison that uses the words "like" or "as" in it.

Here's one:

The desert sand was as hot as a campfire.

Now try coming up with some of your own, and write them in your writer's notebook.

On The Web

Go to http://www.homeschoolshare.com/desert_animals.php for a terrific printable lapbook about deserts. They include lots of desert animals.

SCIENCE: FLUIDS

Fabulous Fact

When a diver is under the water, safety signal flags are used to warn nearby boaters to stay clear of the area.

In the U.S. this flag is used:

In the U.K. it's this one:

Additional Layer

Archimedes said: *Any floating object displaces its own weight of fluid.*

Can you design an experiment to prove or disprove this?

Air and water are both fluids, which means that they flow into the shape of their container. There are many other fluids besides air and water, but these two are the most familiar. There are properties that define fluids including buoyancy, surface tension, density, and pressure.

Buoyancy is the level an object floats at in a liquid.

Surface tension can be seen in the "skin" on top of water. It holds together the molecules of water, one to another.

Density means how close together the molecules are. Density depends on the space available, temperature of the fluid, and the chemical composition of the fluid. A balloon filled with helium is less dense than the surrounding air so the balloon floats. The helium molecules are more spread out than the molecules of the atmosphere. The number of molecules in a given space is the density.

The principles of pressure are what make flight possible among other things. Pressure means how hard something is pushing.

☺ ☺ ☺ EXPERIMENT: Diver

Make a diver. You need a film canister (with a lid) and a large glass or plastic jar. The jar should be transparent. Fill the jar with water. Now put the sealed film canister in the water. What happens?

Next, fill the film canister with water and seal it again. Place it in the jar of water. Now what happens?

Finally, experiment to get just the right amount of water in the film canister to make it float mid-way between the top and bottom of the water in the jar.

Now add salt, a ½ cup or so and stir it into the water.

How does your canister float now? What is different?

The height your canister floats at is its buoyancy. Salt makes the water more dense and increases the buoyancy of the water-filled canister.

☺ ☻ EXPEDITION: Dive Shop
Go visit a scuba diving shop in your town. Ask the dive instructors to tell you what they know about density, buoyancy, and pressure. The number one rule of scuba diving is BREATHE. Ask what would happen to a diver who comes up to the surface holding their breath. Ask what would happen if they took an air-filled water bottle down 20 feet, and then brought it back up to the surface. Listen to some of their dive stories (I've yet to meet the scuba diver who didn't love a chance to tell adventure stories). You'll probably get to take a look at their equipment too. Teenagers may even be able to take a free or inexpensive introductory dive in a local swimming pool.

☺ ☻ EXPERIMENT: Density and Buoyancy
Fill a container, like a glass jar, with water. Test different objects to see if they are buoyant in water. You could try a raisin, a grape, a Lego, a cork, and other things you find around the house. Some things are more buoyant than others because they are more dense. The amount of water displaced must have more density than the object you place in the water. This is Archimedes' Principle.

Now try floating those same objects in cooking oil. What is different this time? Which is more dense – water or oil? Pour some oil into the water to make sure. What happens when you try to float these things in corn syrup?

☺ ☻ EXPERIMENT: Surface Tension
Adhesion happens when molecules of the same type are attracted to one another. Surface tension is adhesion at the surface of a liquid.

1. Fill a cup to the very top with water.

2. Now use an eye dropper to put one drop at a time in the cup until the water bulges over the top.
3. Molecules of water are charged, causing them to cling together, so the water can actually be higher than the top of the cup.

If you put water into a narrow glass container, like a test tube, you can see the water curving up to meet the sides of the glass.

The curve is called a meniscus.

☺ ☻ EXPERIMENT: Floating Needle

If you put a needle in water it will sink, right? Usually, but if you place it very carefully you can make it float. It's still more dense than the water, but the surface tension is enough to keep the needle floating. Try it.

*Tip: the needle and your hand must be dry for this to work.

EXPLANATION: Boats

What would you build a boat out of? Wood? Concrete? Plastic? Steel? Believe it or not there are boats built out of all these things. The boat in the picture to the right is built of concrete. Even though all of them, except the wood, are more dense than water, they can float if they displace more water than they weigh. A concrete or steel boat can float if it has a hollowed out center with high sides. Try building a boat out of wood, paper, or clay.

☺ ☺ ☻ EXPERIMENT: Bubbles

Blow some soap bubbles. What shape are they when they are floating in the air? They are round because surface tension pulls the water molecules into a round shape. Make gigantic bubbles:

1. Mix 2 bottles dish washing liquid, six bottle of glycerin (from the drugstore), and 1 gallon of water.
2. Pour it all into a plastic kiddie pool.
3. Use a hula hoop, or similar round object to use as your "wand." You need to attach two handles to your wand, one on each side. Use pipe cleaners, wire, or string to make small handles.
4. Then pull straight up on the hula hoop from the bubble mixture. You can do it with a partner too.

☺ ☻ EXPERIMENT: Air Lift

Is air strong enough to lift you? Try this: Place a board on a deflated beach ball. Stand on the board above the beach ball. Now inflate the beach ball. Did you rise into the air? Air is actually strong stuff. When the air was forced into the beach ball, the

Explanation

There was a time when I believed in order to educate children I had to touch on everything. . . all the facets of every subject. What if I missed something? What if there were holes in their education? The pressure on me at the beginning of my homeschool journey felt immense and almost unbearable. As I meticulously mapped out our yearly curriculum I had an important moment of realization. I was listing all of the things I had to cover within the topic of Asian geography when it occurred to me that I graduated from an amazing university without knowing much about Asian geography beyond where to find Asia on a map. That's when I realized that DEPTH, INTEREST, and EXCITEMENT are much more key to a child's education than ensuring that every point is covered perfectly. Now I research my overall subjects until I find something that I think the kids will find wildly interesting, and then I take off from there . . .

Karen

Famous Folks

Ernst Mach first investigated the properties of supersonic (faster than the speed of sound) flow. The speed scale based on the speed of sound was named after him.

Additional Layer

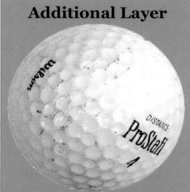

Birds' wings, airplane wings, and golf balls all use Bernoulli's principle in their design. Find out more about how each of these creates lift.

Additional Layer

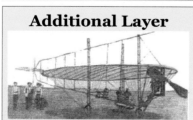

Learn more about the quest for human flight.

molecules of air became closer together or more dense, this is called pressure. We use pressurized air in our bicycle and car tires as well.

☺ ☺ ☺ **EXPERIMENT: Bernoulli's Principle**

Bernoulli's Principle states that moving air has less pressure than still air. Demonstrate this with a piece of paper. Hold the paper in front of your face with the paper parallel to the ground. Let the paper flop toward the ground. Blow on the bottom side of the paper to make it rise. Now try blowing on the top. The lower pressure will create a natural vacuum and lift the paper again.

Now try the same principle with two empty pop cans. Place the pop cans very near each other, but not touching. Blow hard between the two cans. What do you predict will happen? What does happen? How does this demonstrate Bernoulli's principle?

☺ ☺ ☻ EXPERIMENT: Model Airplane Wing

Make a model airplane wing. You need paper, tape, and a fan or hair dryer. Fold a standard size sheet of paper so that one side is shorter by about an inch than the other side. Tape the edges together so they match, one side of the paper must curve. Tie a string onto the taped edge of the paper. Now place it in front of a fan or hairdryer. Blow the air at the straight edge of the paper with the curved paper on top. The air on the top of the wing, the curved part, must travel further than the air on the bottom. This makes the air on top less dense, so the air below pushes up, giving lift to the wings. What happens if you place the straight side of the paper on top?

☺ ☺ ☻ EXPEDITION: Flight museum

Find out if there is a museum or display of flight near you and visit it. If you know any pilots they are typically thrilled to talk about their flying adventures and the physics of flight.

Fabulous Fact

To learn about all these principles of physics in air, scientists first had to create a controlled environment where they could test their hypothesis. They created wind tunnels.

Additional Layer

When air passes across an airplane's curved wing the air flowing over the wing travels faster than the air below the wing. This unequal speed causes a vortex of swirling air to come off the wing. In this picture from NASA an airplane has flown through a cloud of colored smoke to show the vortex.

Famous Folks

Learn more about the first successful pilots, the Wright Brothers.

THE ARTS: RHYTHM

Additional Layer
These children's books all have great rhythm:

Fiddle I Fee by Will Hillenbrand

The Owl and the Pussy Cat by Edward Lear, ill. By Jan Brett

Clickety Clack by Robert Spence III

Barnyard Banter by Denise Fleming

Bee-bim Bop by Linda Sue Park

Clap and chant to the rhythm of these books with your little ones. You can also use nursery rhyme verses.

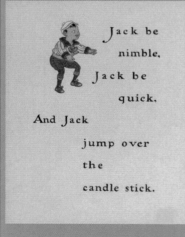

Jack be nimble, Jack be quick, And Jack jump over the candle stick.

Additional Layer

Sing *If You're Happy and You Know It* using new made-up body rhythms in place of the "clap your hands."

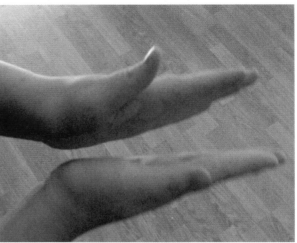

We can hear rhythm all around us. Clapping hands, falling rain, a basketball being dribbled, feet walking along the sidewalk – if you're listening for it, you can hear rhythm almost anywhere. Simply put, rhythm is the timing of musical sounds. It's the pulse of the music. It's made up of sounds and silences that create repeated patterns. Often rhythms have a steady beat that repeats itself, but this is not always true. In just one song, you may hear many different rhythms.

☺ ☻ **EXPLORATION: Rhythm Imitators**
Clap a simple rhythm, then have the kids mimic the rhythm. They should clap at the same speed and to the same beat. Begin by keeping the rhythm short and simple—just 4 beats is a fine place to start. Once they've mastered the beat, show them how to lengthen the rhythm by repeating it over and over again. Do the same 4 beats twice or three times in a row to make 8 or 12 beats.

Once they get really good, make the rhythms longer and trickier and try to fool them! You can even combine clapping with stomping, hitting a table, or playing on a percussion instrument. Make it into a game. Start with everyone echoing the rhythms, and if they make a mistake they have to sit down. The last one standing wins!

☺ ☻ **EXPLORATION: Body Percussion**
We can keep a beat on almost anything. Use only your body and see how many rhythmic sounds you can create. Some may be extremely quiet while others will be much louder.

☺ ☻ ☻ **EXPLORATION: Karaoke Drummer**
Play some music that has a good beat to it. Faster, up tempo pieces work the best. Try to "play along" with the drummer. You may be playing on the beat, playing on the off-beat (much harder), or playing alternating beats. Often rock and pop songs

have multiple drummers, or at least multiple beats. You don't need to follow them exactly, as long as you find a working beat within the music.

*For young ones, this may just be an activity in noise. That's okay. If they are able, they may be able to follow a simple rhythm you find in the song (like just playing on the strongest downbeat) and "make noise" with you. As kids get older and grow in musical experience and coordination, they are typically more able to find patterns and rhythms within the music.

☻ ☻ EXPLORATION: Reading Rhythm

In Western music, rhythm is based on time signatures in music. The time signature is just a set of numbers at the beginning of a song that tell you how many beats will be in each meter of the song. For example, in the picture below, the time signature is 3/4. This means that there are 3 quarter notes per measure, or meter. The 3 denotes the number of notes, and the 4 shows the type of note, in this case, a quarter note (which is a basic note that gets 1 count).

Many other cultures don't use this kind of notation at all. African drummers are known for their rhythmic abilities, and they don't use the western system. One popular rhythm notation among drummers is the Djembe notation:

D: Dun ("Doon")=bass beat with left hand	
G: Gun ("Goon")=bass beat with right hand	
d: do ("doe")=rim beat with left hand	
g: go=rim beat with right hand	
T: Ta=slap beat with left hand: sharp glancing stroke	
P: Pa=slap beat with right hand	
- = space	

A piece of music using the Djembe notation might look like this:

D - D - d g d g
Dun *(rest)* **Dun** *(rest)* **do go do go**

Can you play that beat?

Explanation
Listening to music should not just be reserved for "music class." Most kids learn really well when appropriate music is played in the background. Classical music while studying math facts helps many kids retain the information much more completely.

Playing an upbeat number to move and dance to provides a great break when you've expected quiet for awhile. We often turn up the tunes after silent reading.

Additional Layer
Performing in front of an audience is a great experience for kids. Prepare and practice a rhythm song or two for several weeks and plan for an opportunity to perform them. Don't forget to explain to children what their behavior should be like during a performance and decide ahead of time how the performers should dress.

There are also a great many drummers who don't follow a notation at all. They just have music within them and can feel and play the beat.

☺ ☻ EXPLORATION: Homemade Percussion
The great thing about percussion instruments is that most of them are tune free. Although they have different sounds, most aren't a specific pitch (timpani drums, bells, glockenspiels, xylophones, and vibraphones are the exceptions). Because they don't need to be tuned or carry a specific pitch, they are very easy to make. There are even popular bands and famous musicians that use everyday items like garbage cans as drums. Find at least four things around your home that you can use as a drum. Also find at least four household items to use as mallets. Experiment a bit with your sounds. Does the sound change depending on the mallet you use?

☺ ☻ EXPLORATION: Coffee Can Drum
To make a coffee can drum you'll need to gather:
*   an empty coffee can
*   2 round pieces of leather (real or faux works), about 10 inches in diameter
*   string or twine
*   a pair of scissors

Using the scissors, cut small round holes around the outside edges of the leather circles, about every 3 inches apart. Stretch the circles over each side of the coffee can. Lace the twine through the holes you created and lace it through, weaving up and down to secure the leather on the ends of the can. Once you've gone through each hole, tie the twine off to itself.

You can play the drum with your hands or you can create mallets for it using wooden dowels with a square of felt filled with cotton balls tied on to the end with a piece of yarn.

☺ ☻ EXPLORATION: Rhythm Charts
Copy a rhythm chart below for each musician. In the spaces below, write which instruments you are using. These could be real instruments like a hand drum, triangle, or tambourine, or you could use any of the homemade percussion instruments you've created. You could also just assign one person to clap, one to pat their legs or stomp, and one to snap. Using real or homemade

ythm Charts

ted lines. Fill in your own instrument names and create

percussion instruments, perform a beat using the rhythm chart. The song won't have a melody line, but the various sounds of percussion instruments will make for a unique sound. It helps a lot if you have one person to act as the conductor who keeps the overall 1, 2, 3, 4 beat with his or her hand or a baton.

Additional Layer
American slave children used to sing hand clapping rhymes while they worked.

Instrument	1	2	3	4	1	2	3	4	1	2	3	4	1	2	3	4
		X		X		X		X	X	X	X		X		X	
			X		X		X		X				X		X		X
		X	X			X	X			X	X			X	X	

Next, have the students compose their own rhythm charts. They can have it be purely beats, or they begin with a familiar song and then add beats to it. They can just do one line for one instrument or add multiple instruments and beats. Well-known folk songs work really well for this. Try *Go Tell Aunt Rhodie*; *Skip To My Lou*; *Twinkle, Twinkle Little Star*; or *Yankee Doodle*. You'll find a blank rhythm charts template in the printables section.

☺ ☺ ☺ **EXPLORATION: Rhythm Relay**
This game is played like Telephone. All the players line up in a line. The first player taps a rhythm on the shoulder of the person next to them; that person taps the same rhythm on the next player's shoulder; and it continues down the line until the end. The last person demonstrates the rhythm for everyone. You try to pass it all the way down the line without anyone changing the rhythm. For a more difficult game, create 2 lines. You'll basically play the same way, except make it a race to see who can get down their line the fastest with the correct rhythm.

☺ ☺ ☺ **EXPLORATION: Clapping Game**
Children all over the world do hand clapping games to a rhythm. Below we give three common rhymes. Make up your own hand

Additional Layer

Try using hand clapping or marching to a beat to help you memorize a favorite poem. This will work if the poem has a definite meter.

Spelling words can also be done this way. Jump rope and beanbag spelling are our favorites. You engage more of your brain by moving and incorporating rhythm while you learn. Just keep a beat while chanting the spellings and either jumping rope or throwing a beanbag.

clapping rhythm, whether alone or with a partner.

Additional Layer
The Mary Mack rhyme dates back at least to the American Civil War and possibly refers to an ironclad ship called the Merrimack.

Additional Layer
Jump roping is often done to rhymes like these as well. Try it.

On The Web
Go to YouTube and search for *Stomp* or *The Blue Man Group*. Both music groups use rhythm and percussion in very unique ways.

Oh, Mary Mack Mack Mack
all dressed in black black black
with silver buttons buttons buttons
all down her back back back
She asked her mother mother mother
for fifty cents cents cents
to see an elephant elephant elephant
jump over the fence fence fence
He jumped so high high high
he reached the sky sky sky
and didn't come back back back
til the fourth of July ly ly

. . . .

Down by the banks of the Hanky Panky
Where the bullfrogs jump from bank to banky
Where the eeps, ops, sodapops
Hey Mr. Lilypad and went kerplops.

. . . .

A sailor went to sea sea sea
To see what he could see see see
And all that he could see see see
Was the bottom of the deep blue sea sea sea.

Coming up next. . .
Unit I-9
Persians – Arctic
Waves – Melody

My Ideas For This Unit:

Title: _____   Topic: _____

_____

_____

_____

_____

_____

_____

_____

_____

Title: _____   Topic: _____

_____

_____

_____

_____

_____

_____

_____

_____

Title: _____   Topic: _____

_____

_____

_____

_____

_____

_____

_____

_____

My Ideas For This Unit:

Title: _____   Topic: _____

_____

_____

_____

_____

_____

_____

_____

_____

_____

Title: _____   Topic: _____

_____

_____

_____

_____

_____

_____

_____

_____

_____

_____

Title: _____   Topic: _____

_____

_____

_____

_____

_____

_____

_____

_____

Assyrian Lamassu

A lamassu was a protector god of the ancient Assyrians. It was the body of a bull with wings and the head of a man. Lamassu statues guarded many important places.

Assyrians: Unit I-8

2000 BC

Assyrian Kingdom established

1220 BC

Babylon comes under the control of Assyria

1000-663 BC

Assyrian Kingdom grows into an empire

883-859 BC

King Ashurbanipal II is king of Assyria, and the city of Nimrud is built

841 BC

Israel is paying tribute to Assyria

704-681 BC

King Sennacherib builds Nineveh

701 BC

Sennacherib defeats most of Israel, but fails to take the capital city, Jerusalem

671 BC

Assyrians conquer Egypt

612-609 BC

Babylonians and Medes defeat Assyria at Carchemish and the empire falls.

Make your Own Mythical Guardian

Many peoples throughout the ages have combined a number of beasts together to make formidable creatures like the sphinx and the lamassu. Draw your own creature to guard your bedroom. In the box, write about your creation and the significance of the animals you chose to include.

Description of my guardian:

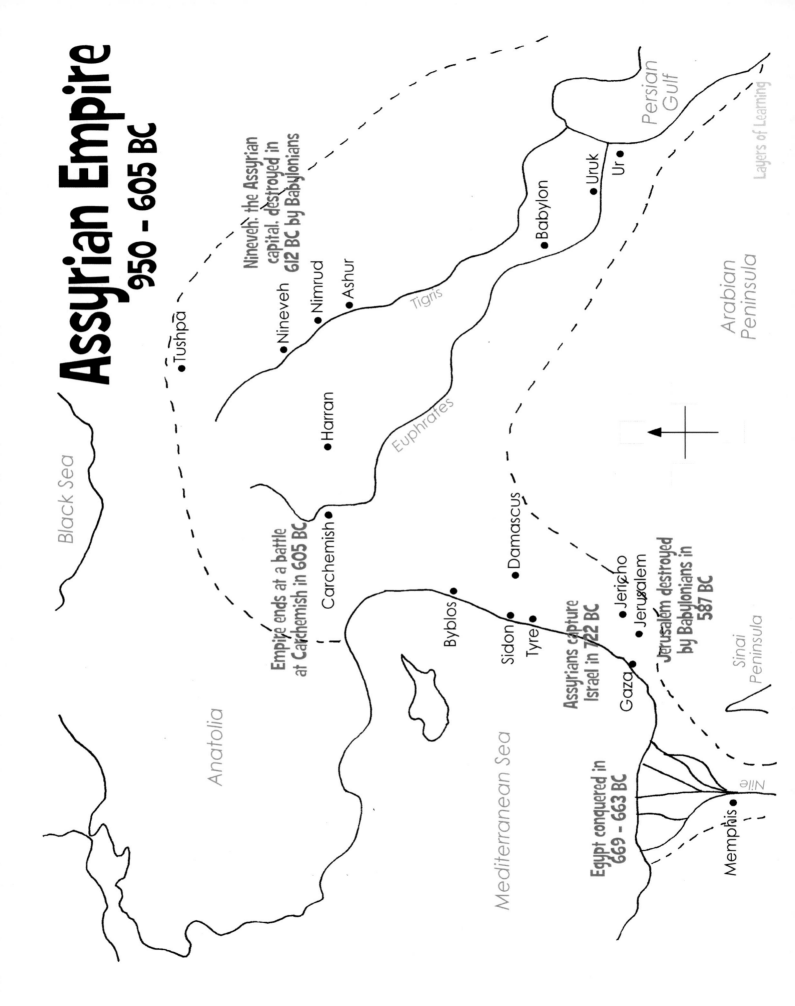

Assyrian Empire
950 - 605 BC

Black Sea

Anatolia

Tushpa

Nineveh: the Assyrian capital, destroyed in 612 BC by Babylonians

Nineveh

Nimrud

Ashur

Tigris

Harran

Euphrates

Babylon

Uruk

Ur

Persian Gulf

Empire ends at a battle at Carchemish in 605 BC

Carchemish

Mediterranean Sea

Byblos

Sidon

Tyre

Damascus

Assyrians capture Israel in 722 BC

Jericho

Jerusalem

Gaza

Jerusalem destroyed by Babylonians in 587 BC

Arabian Peninsula

Egypt conquered in 669 - 663 BC

Sinai Peninsula

Nile

Memphis

Layers of Learning

Library Scavenger Hunt

Find all 15 items

A cookbook

A book about an artist

A book from the 921 non-fiction section

A board book for babies

An atlas

A fairy tale

A graphic novel

A medieval history book

Someone typing on a computer

Your favorite book

A science book

A sci-fi book about space

A clock

A library card

An encyclopedia set

Layers of Learning

Deserts of the World

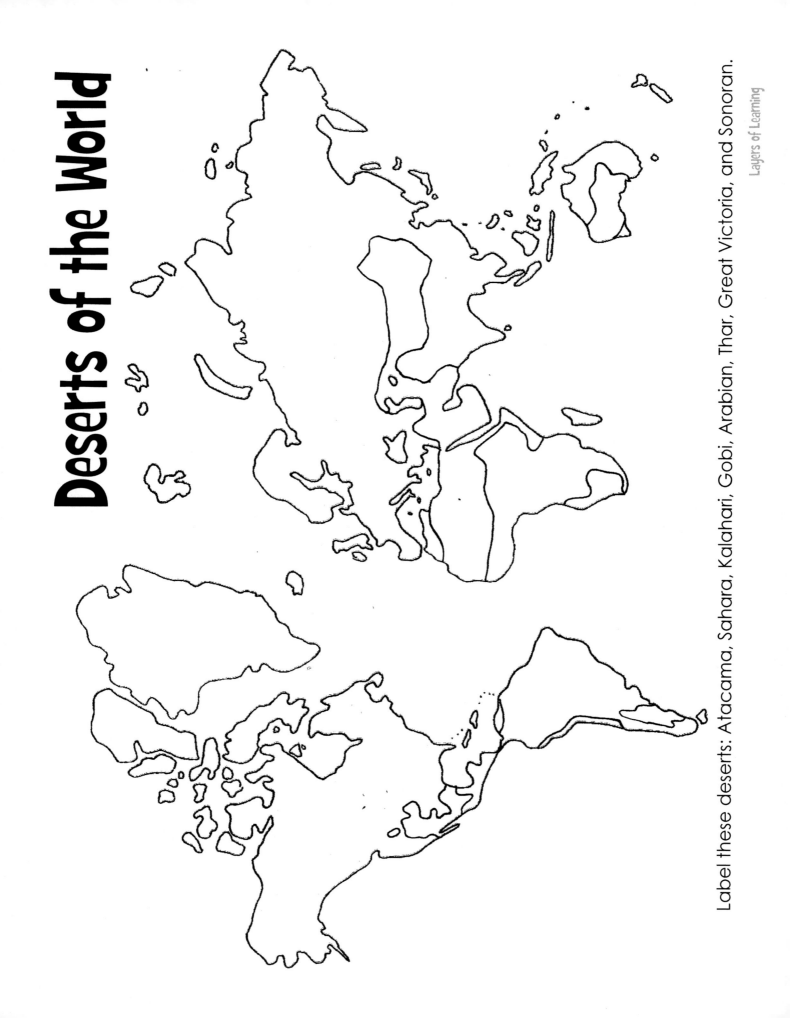

Label these deserts: Atacama, Sahara, Kalahari, Gobi, Arabian, Thar, Great Victoria, and Sonoran.

Deserts

Plants of the Desert

Animals of the Desert

People and Homes of the Desert

Rhythm Charts

Cut apart the page at the dotted lines. Fill in your own instrument names and create rhythm patterns to play.

- - - - - - - - - - - - - - - -

Instrument	1	2	3	4	1	2	3	4	1	2	3	4	1	2	3	4

- - - - - - - - - - - - - - - -

Instrument	1	2	3	4	1	2	3	4	1	2	3	4	1	2	3	4

- - - - - - - - - - - - - - - -

Instrument	1	2	3	4	1	2	3	4	1	2	3	4	1	2	3	4

- - - - - - - - - - - - - - - -

Instrument	1	2	3	4	1	2	3	4	1	2	3	4	1	2	3	4

ABOUT THE AUTHORS

Karen & Michelle . . .
Mothers, sisters, teachers, women who are passionate
about educating kids.
We are dedicated to lifelong learning.

Karen, a mother of four, who has homeschooled her kids for more than eight years with her husband, Bob, has a bachelor's degree in child development with an emphasis in education. She lives in Utah where she gardens, teaches piano, and plays an excruciating number of board games with her kids. Karen is our resident Arts expert and English guru {most necessary as Michelle regularly and carelessly mangles the English language and occasionally steps over the bounds of polite society}.

Michelle and her husband, Cameron, homeschooling now for over a decade, teach their six boys on their ten acres in beautiful Idaho country. Michelle earned a bachelor's in biology, making her the resident Science expert, though she is mocked by her friends for being the *Botanist with the Black Thumb of Death*. She also is the go-to for History and Government. She believes in staying up late, hot chocolate, and a no whining policy. We both pitch in on Geography, in case you were wondering, and are on a continual quest for knowledge.

Visit our constantly updated blog for tons of free ideas,
free printables, and more cool stuff for sale:
www.Layers-of-Learning.com